DEAD
LOVE

Also by Wade Walker

CODE NAME: LONEWOLF THRILLERS

BITE

OF THE

WOLF

AND

OPERATION

FRANKENSTEIN

APOCALYPTIC POP SONNETS

WADE WALKER

World Mythic Entertainment

World Mythic Entertainment

First printing, October 2025

ISBN: 979-8-9871084-6-8

PRE-MORTEM

The poems that comprise this collection originated as songs, so they aren't poems with a capital "P," per se—at least not in the traditional sense of meter or form. They were composed for melody, for verse-chorus-verse, making many of them closer to incantations, especially with the repeated choruses.

Still, I felt they worked in a poetic sense. Some liberties were taken with the original lyrics where necessary to better fit a more poetic meter and style. As it's been said, *"Poetry is delivered to the eye, while lyrics are delivered to the ear."* Speaking of taking liberties, traditionally, sonnets are 14-line poems. A couple of pieces in this collection happen to fit that definition, but most wander beyond it or fall short of it. I've used the word "sonnets" here in a looser, pop-apocalyptic sense: part homage, part cheekiness, and perhaps more than a dollop of willful ignorance.

While compiling the poems, I came across another axiom: *"You should always separate a writer's work from his persona."* I do think this is generally true. And certainly, when it comes to sordid verses about the joys of necrophilia or the "well-wishes" of a spurned would-be lover for his intended to be hacked to pieces and tossed in a river—yes, I'd say that most definitely applies to me. *(note: this is not me over-insisting… I think.)*

These things do come from somewhere, of course, but I'm afraid the less interesting and less psychoanalytical answer is that, while some parts are personal, most are simply imaginative fiction, borne of a lifetime absorbing horror flicks, classic gothic tales, the macabre, dark lyricism, and the works of master poets like Edgar Allan Poe. But most of all, they come from an overactive—if not over-morbid and tastelessly lurid—imagination.

Some of these pieces—particularly the early ones—are almost wholesomely earnest. Take *Take Me Down* (please!), or middle-period entries like *I've Come to Kiss You*. What stood out to me in reviewing these as a whole was the persistent undercurrent of something bent—something (even if just a little) off-kilter. This comes from my appreciation of song lyrics and poetry where even a single line or word can make something seemingly romantic suddenly feel sinister. It adds a wrinkle that invites a second look, seen in a different and darker light.

Can you hear it? On the surface, it's just a sweet, seemingly innocuous little pop song. But then… wait—did they really say *that*? Some little dark nugget that shifts the entire thing, that undermines, in the best way, all the lovey-dovey sugar words you just heard or read. It breathes new life—or, maybe more appropriately, turns it into a vampire of lyricism. Something that only inhabits what it first appeared to be.

These poems were written starting in my teenage years, through my twenties, into my thirties, and… well, we'll stop there. Just know that they run the range of most of my adult life, reflecting different seasons of thought, influence, and voice. *Dead Love* also breaks new ground with what may be the first-ever instrumental poem. You heard it here first… or did you?

Yes, there are touches—some overt, some covert—of necrophilia, the love of the dead, but that isn't necessarily what the title *Dead Love* is all about. In a broader context, it's about love that's lost, love that's irreparably broken, love that is eternally unrequited and unrecognized—a dead love that, much like dead eyes, has nothing left behind it. Just a lonely soul holding on to love that never lived, a love they will take to the grave, where maybe, finally, they'll find an embrace that won't let go.

So curl up with your love on a cold autumn night, and leaf through these lines before you close the lid tight.

Wade Walker
Location Undisclosed
October 2025

DEAD LOVE

APOCALYPTIC POP SONNETS

EYES OF FIRE

Beautiful ageless people in satin sheets
on a hot, windy night —
translucent youth, years and years,
deep crimson feelings of flowing life.

Looks that burn, heads that turn,
you've seen her, you walked right by her —

She's the girl with the eyes of fire.

Believe in sweet tastes, like fine wine,
as long midnights gently roll by —

striking intensified eyes,

moonglow faces and hormonal sighs.

Looks that burn, heads that turn,

you've seen her, you walked right by her —

She's the girl with the eyes of fire.

She's the girl with the eyes of fire.

Burning, turning,

burning eyes of fire.

I'VE COME TO KISS YOU

I've come to kiss you —
that's what I'm here to do.
I've come to kiss you —
hope you wanna kiss me, too.

I'm not just the boy next door,
the one you always ignore.
Kiss you like you never been kissed before.

Oh yeah, yeah —
you're so sweet.
Oh yeah, yeah —

soon we will meet.
Oh yeah.

Sun sets, the moon rises high —
1990s springtime sky.
Tonight's the night, it feels so right,
and I've come here to kiss you tonight.

Oh yeah, yeah —
you're so sweet.
Oh yeah, yeah —
meet me in the street.
Oh yeah.

Make me smile, you're my Zoloft.
Inhaled your air when you coughed.
You're a place for my heart to crash —
and I'm the nice guy who won't finish last.

I've come to kiss you —
that's what I'm here to do.
I've come to kiss you —
hope you wanna kiss me, too.

Oh yeah, yeah —
you're so sweet.
Oh yeah, yeah —
hearts will beat.
Kiss me in the street.

Oh yeah, yeah
I've come to kiss you
I'm here to kiss you
Oh…
Yeah.

SHE'S 22

She was a brainchild, a real Jane Child —
she even had that little chain thing.
When she walked by, over to some guy,
I saw the glistening of her tongue ring.

She's 22, la, la, la.
When she talks it's blah, blah, blah.

I'm ready,
I'm waiting,
I'm ass-gyrating.

Like an Asgardian angel,

and just about as attainable.

Underground sweet desire, that's real.

God send me this pill-poppin' princess,

look-a-like Juliana Hatfield.

With a bathroom high, a shiver and a sigh,

strike up an innocent conversation —

will it bring a new night of exclamation,

or the usual empty bottle of antici… pation?

She's 22, la, la, la.

When she talks it's blah, blah, blah.

Broken hearts want broken necks.

She's 22, la, la, la.

When she talks it's blah, blah, blah.

She can't wait to break my heart.

She's 22 and waiting for me.

She's a tube and a real beauty.

She showed me her wound — isn't it good?

I did what any Norwegian would.

She's 22.

La, la, la.

Blah, blah, blah.

EVERYDAY EYES

Never seen a smile like yours,

and eyes so right.

Am I even in your line of sight?

The ugly lights come on, *Closing Time* plays —

and you're still a beauty in every crazy way.

Looking at you with everyday eyes.

Soul's window, telling no lies.

Your eyes are pools of bright-light jewels.

Yours aren't no everyday eyes, baby —

yours are no everyday eyes.

The eyes have it, they saw that I fell.

You're a little devil, teasing me to hell.

Heartbeats bleating outside of the bar —

we kissed in the street beneath autumn stars.

You ask if you're pretty, and I say yes —

and tasting pretty good is beer on your breasts.

Our eyes connect, and I have to confess:

Listen, baby, I'm not telling no lies.

Look at the truth in my everyday eyes.

Looking at you with everyday eyes.

Soul's window, telling no lies.

Your eyes are pools of bright-light jewels.

Yours aren't no everyday eyes, baby —

yours are no everyday eyes.

Yours are no everyday eyes.

SHADOWED BY YOUR BEAUTY

Traipsing through the yard with you
upon this autumn eve —
the beautiful ones, who've come to love
where others come to grieve.

Tripping over a stone,
with a lovers' laugh we fall down.
With you laying over me,
and the spirits all around.

Shadowed by your beauty.
Shadowed by your beauty.

By the pale blue light of the moon.
In the pale blue light of the moon.

A-fucking away in the evening grass,
starlit dew upon your cheek.
A-fucking away in our midnight mass —
so lovely, so dark, so deep.

Morbid delight, O' our sweet
grave-candle lit lust.
Poems carved in stone that tonight
were meant just for us.

Amongst the catacombs, where we roam,
we take this night as ours —
two broken blossoms in nightly bloom,
sacred love in the secret hours.

As we lay ourselves in dark caress,
we will warm this icy womb.
For tonight, my love, as I rest upon your breast,
this tomb is our bedroom.

Shadowed by your beauty.

Shadowed by your beauty.

By the pale blue light of the moon.

In the pale blue light of the moon.

MANDY, IT'S ONLY YOU

Mandy, after all the hate,

love is so sweet.

I fell in love when I heard your name.

Every day without you

is more incomplete.

After you, nothing was the same.

Mandy, it's only you.

Only you, only you.

Mandy, it's only you.

Only you, only you, my dancing fool.

Mandy, it was only you
from the first time.
You know we could not escape too soon.
And I can't even look you in the eyes —
you had me mourning in the afternoon.

Mandy, was it the end
when we said goodnight?
I was so scared of going alone.
But Mandy, if you go,
I want you to know
that what you stole has left me cold.

Mandy, without you in my life,
I didn't know if I could go on.
But now your letters are burning bright,
and the last of you is almost gone.

Mandy, it's only you.
Only you, only you.
Mandy, it's only you.
Only you, only you, my dancing fool.

TAKE ME DOWN

Whenever I see her go on by,
I get shivers all up and down my spine.
Today is a good day, I can tell —
maybe today you can give me hell.

Take me down, take me down.
Take me down, to you.

Tell me — where is your bird now?
Is it still singing, is it staying around?
Look at the sky, tell me what you see.
When you see a cloud, think of me.

Wherever she goes, so do I.

This time around, I won't have to lie.

Don't have to be the fool, and act the clown —

this time I know she's taken me down.

Take me down, take me down.

Take me down, to you.

UNDYING IS AN ART

I'll claw my way up through this dirt,
Six feet and rising through this earth.
Now I've broken free of my tomb,
And here I stand within your room.

I come before you as your corpse groom,
To embrace you under the blood moon.
Your breath catches, but you do not run,
You knew this night would surely come.

You lit the candle, spoke the vow,
And I am what you summoned now.

Though cold my touch, my love burns hot,
Flee my reach, you say, "Touch me not."

Still I drag you to my plot,
Into the soil, love forever forgot.

Back to my grave, where we both can rot.

BIRD

Is there a second chance,
or is this my last dance?
Oh, how I've taken for granted
the things that have happened.

Fly bird, fly, oh.
Time to say goodbye, no.
Little bird, fly away —
I'll see you again one day.

Is there another way
to stop what happened today?

That's not my greatest fear —
that I might disappear.

When the last bird has taken flight
and I'm lost in the night,
what can I say, what is the word
to wing you back, my preying bird?

Has she returned to me,
so hazy, as if a dream
Day or night, I'll wait at home —
either by myself or all alone.

Fly bird, fly, oh.
Time to say goodbye, no.
Blurred bird, fly away —
I'll see you again one day.

CHEMICALS

Chemicals, chemicals.
Lovely, lovely chemicals.
Chemicals, chemicals.
Everybody do chemicals.

Chemicals, chemicals.
Lots and lots of chemicals.
All the chemicals that you see,
all the chemicals that are in your cupboards —
even the ones that aren't in your cupboards—
Do them anyway.

Chemicals, chemicals.

Lovely, lovely chemicals.

We are heavy into chemicals.

Chemicals, chemicals.

Lovely, lovely chemicals.

The Beatles are heavy into chemicals.

Chemicals, chemicals.

Lovely, lovely chemicals.

CHEMICALS

MAGICKAL SPARKLING KISS

There's nowhere to run and hide —
my feelings committed suicide.
Of all the winds that twist and twirl,
did I find a love that whirls?

She would know that I was here,
if I knew that she were near.
Will things always be like this?
She's a magickal sparkling kiss.

I'm so confused — I like it that way.
I try to get found every day.

Sit on a bench, watch the world go by —
all I'm seeing is her, my, my, my, my.

She would know that I was here,
if I knew that she were near.
Will things always be like this?
She's a magickal sparkling kiss.

Let me tell you that love is the same,
no matter how it's spelled.
Hours and times and weeks and days —
now everyone knows how far I fell.

She would know that I was here,
if I knew that she were near.
Will things always be like this?
She's a magickal sparkling kiss.

THERE WILL BE LOVE TONIGHT

You… and I… will come.
There will be love tonight.
You — yeah, you… will find.
There will be love tonight.

Ballin' it, I'm callin' it, your naughty bits,
it's on tonight, we two.
Take me home for a dirty hour —
dirty like dirty doo-doo, do, awhoo.

Like a beast in the night,
I howl with delight.
Necromancer, neck-romancing you.

You — yeah, you, have a heart of cash.
How can you spend a broken heart?

You, no you… you and I will come.
And there will be love tonight.
Right? Right, right?
There will be love tonight.

CRAZY BEAST

Left my heart hanging around your neck.
Hold my head up, but I'm still a wreck.
Head in hand, now I'm the stupid man —
learn to pick myself up again.

Thought I was over you, not in the least.
I'm still in love with you, you crazy beast.
Thought I was over you, not in the least.
I'm still in love with you, you crazy beast.

You love your horror movies.
I love my cemeteries.

You love your karaoke —
but you don't love me.
You don't love me.

Though I have no heart to break no more,
I could kiss her lips and still feel yours.
You're a curse of the worst, the eternal kind —
everyday forever, on my mind.

Thought I was over you, not in the least.
I'm still in love with you, you crazy beast.
Thought I was over you, not in the least.
I'm still in love with you, you crazy beast.

Damn you to hell, you crazy fucking beast.

I'VE HEART ENOUGH

I've heart enough—my pulse has gone deaf.
Look like hell
and smell like shit—
half-baked living death.

Living through this is killing me,
can't get over my obsession,
with my own depression.

I'm a Buddhist procrastinator— I keep putting things
off until the next life.

Why do today what I might not have to do at all,
should the atheists be proven right.

Truth is subject to change, time dies,
brought to you by my mind's eyes.

A long and dreamed existence,
like a phoenix rising from the ash,
only to get burnt again,
a non-flame retarded,
endlessly tragic ass.

At least I'm a real monster,
made of leather,
stitched together.
The sum of my spirit is greater
than that of my bag of moans.
Though hell would bar the way,
I will reclaim my soul.

Delicate creatures, cloned from the bones—
my favorite ugly things,
newly in the throes of love,
grounded, bound by broken wings.

Life's like a box of poisonous snakes,

a low rustling through last year's dead leaves.

I prayed for you by mistake,

Nice gods finish last, irredeemably deceived.

Mistake me for who you will.

Everything has changed,

my smile now has fangs.

I've heart enough, now throw the bones,

piss and cast them out as broken, galled stones.

I held you up like a wrought-iron gate

that opens to my road.

Danger ahead — bridge out — point of no return.

Road Closed.

NOBODY PUTS BABY IN A CORNER

I want your habit.

I want to have it —

a little bit o' the insane

crawling deep, back in my brain.

Nobody puts baby in a corner.

Nobody puts baby in a corner —

because I'm a maniac for her.

Like a summer cemetery,

I've got a peaceful, sleazy feeling.

A delicious prize, unwon
by desire for the stealing.

She says "stab," I stab.
She says "kill," I kill.
She says "dress like a girl, like Milton Berle."
She drags me to a bathroom world.

Nobody puts baby in a corner.
Nobody puts baby in a corner —
because I'm a maniac for her.

Because I'm a maniac for her.
I'm a maniac for her.

Nobody puts baby in a corner

LIGHT A CANDLE FOR LILLIAN

Light a candle for Lillian —
this beauty, she has just died,
away to such a warm, lovely place.
I'll be on my way soon, in time.

I keep falling when I think of you,
turning, twisting like a storm on the ocean.
No, you're not only sleeping —
I'm holding you in slow motion.

Light a candle for Lillian.
Hold it true as you look at her face.

One unbroken feeling —
oh, the sadness in this place.

You can feel her in the breeze.
I can hear her sing to me.
Light a candle for Lillian,
and kiss her sweet face goodbye.

Sweet fragrance, dead flowers in the air —
so many tears have been cried.
Lying there upon that bed,
the last time you closed your eyes.

I keep falling when I think of you —
your cup has runneth over in my hand.
I'll be waiting here for you,
as my hourglass drains of sand.

Light a candle for Lillian.
Hold it true as you look at her face.
One unbroken feeling —
oh, the sadness in this place.

You can feel her in the breeze.

I can hear her sing to me.

Oh, light a candle for Lillian,

and kiss her sweet lips goodbye.

BAD FOR YOU

After the way I've treated you,
after the way that I have been —
progressive entrapment, it seems,
is now what I am in.

Weird vibes and bad times,
you're still on my mind.
I've got it bad for you.

Nowhere to go and nothing to show —
now I think that everyone knows.

That's good for me,
and bad for you.

I know you've heard all this before.
It's in everything you will hear.
Less is a lot less, and less is more.
Feelin' blue, what can I do, oh dear.

Weird vibes and tan lines,
you're still on my mind.
I've got it bad for you.

Nowhere to go and nothing to show —
now I think that everyone knows.
That's good for me,
and bad for you.

Analyze the frequency,
day-in, day-out, today.
Oh, you awesomely beautiful
worldly nectar babes.

Weird vibes and bad times,
you're still on my mind.
I've got it bad for you.

Nowhere to go and nothing to show —
now I think that everyone knows.
That's good for me,
and bad for you.

Bad for you, baybay.
Bad for you, baybay.
Bad for you, baybay.

COLD STARE

Let me throw you down some damage, baby

Maybe it's the labia

That cold stare

That lustful glare

Baby, I don't care—

I don't care that you're a compulsive liar

You set my heart and my house on fire

One sweet li'l pyromaniac

One day I'll kill you

and turn necrophiliac

I'm pleading, babe

Please plead me, oh yeah

Pleading the Fifth for you

BURY ME

Bury me in the ground,
and I'll lay here forever.
I said, "Never say die,"
and now I just say "Never."

I'll float and blow the candles you have lit out.
I'll appear in your house and throw your dishes about.

Bury me upside up or upside down, underground —
then come trample my grave while you dance around.

Bury me, then come plant a flower on my grave, and wish,
like you would plant a kiss upon my lips.

Hand over hand, in a perfumed shroud,
as the worm turns in my burial mound.

Bury me deep, and roses will grow from my bones.
Bury me deep, so I don't try to come home.

I'll float and blow the candles you have lit out.
I'll appear in your house and throw your dishes about.

Bury me, then come dance on my grave, and piss —
after all, that was your one and only wish.

GO AHEAD, BABY

Go ahead, baby.

Let him sweet talk you a while.

Let him win you with his smile.

Let him have this dance.

Let him win, let him take my chance.

Go ahead, baby.

Go ahead, baby.

But when you're with him, remember —

you could have gone with me.

You could have gone with me.

Go ahead, baby.

Let him take you home.

Let him get in your pants.

Let him smack you when you're alone.

Let him cut you while you watch.

Let him shove shards of glass up your crotch.

Let him slap you with demands.

Let him choke you with your own hands.

Go ahead, baby.

Go ahead, baby.

But when you're with him, remember —

you could have gone with me.

You could have gone with me.

Go ahead, baby.

Let him have orgasmic bliss.

Let him gut you like a fish.

Let him write on you with his dick.

Let him wrap you in plastic.

Let him watch your final death shiver.

Let him toss you like trash into the river.

Let him watch you sink like a stone.

Let him laugh on, all the way home.

Go ahead, baby.

Go ahead, baby.

But when you're with him, remember —

you could have gone with me.

You could have gone with me.

Now you're long gone, gone.

Gone away from me.

BURN

I've been alone —

no one's fault but my own.

And you won't hear regret in my voice.

I know that I will wait.

Don't know the time or date —

and that's all part of my choice.

You burn in my heart.

You're always burning in my heart.

And that's all right with me.

I'll just wait for something,

for someone, to come along.

Until then, I'll just keep going on.

I don't want to have to care,

because then I'd have to share —

and I'm in love with myself.

But if I were to love you,

and it changed all that I knew,

then maybe I could care for someone else.

You burn in my heart.

You're always burning in my heart.

And that's all right with me.

That's all right with me.

NO PRUDES

You can take your promise rings
and put 'em with your other useless things.
I'm a natural-born world shaker,
and a real low-down promise breaker.
And baby, you've been acting like a Quaker.

No time for prudes.
No time for you.
No time for prudes, baby baby —
no time for you.

Baby, you think I'll wait for you?
Oh honey, that just ain't true.
You know I got a lotta living to do —
let's turn the corner,
let's turn the screw.

Soup to nuts, nuts to taint —
you think you're wild child, but you ain't.
Take the padlock off your pants,
throw the key away and assume the stance.
And while you're at it, throw away the "I can'ts."

I'll tell you what's the matter now —
chastity-tising me with your little vow.
Your puri-tyrannical attitude
is killing my mood.
Don't need no prude.

No time for prudes.
No time for you.

No time for prudes, baby baby —
no time for you.

Dear prudes — won't you come out to play?

THE PUMPKIN MAN

There's a man in my house.
There's a man in my house.
There's a man in my house.
What kind of man?

The Pumpkin Man, the Pumpkin Man,
the Pumpkin, Pumpkin, Pumpkin Man.

Everybody do the Pumpkin Man Dance.
Pumpkin Man.

There's a man sitting on my head,
and he's making me eat Pez.

There's a man sitting on my head,

and he's making me eat Pez.

What kind of man is this?

The Pumpkin Man, the Pumpkin Man,

the Pumpkin, Pumpkin, Pumpkin Man.

Everybody do the Pumpkin Man Dance.

Pumpkin Man.

Pumpkin Man.

All hail the Pumpkin Man

ARTIFICIAL FAVOR

Chocolate-covered chariots,
my midnight confections.

When I tell all the world
of your candy-coated kiss —
it's delish.

Candy darling, candy twitch,
must be the raisin of the witch.

The ultimate bubble,
the ultimate trouble,

the ultimate flavor,
the ultimate savior.

You know what I want,
and I know how you get it.

You're just too sweet —
you rot my teeth,
like a cavity creep.

Sugar baby, sugar bum rush.
California creamin'.
You're my candy crush.

CONT-ROL

You're the one I've seen, in all my dreams —
and in my nightmares, too.
My waking hours are not what they seem,
when all I do is written by you.

Standing somewhere in confusion's sea,
in a battle for my very soul.
Cryin' in the wild — won't you rescue me?
Don't you know I'm being cont-rolled?

A surrendered offender
Betrayed.

Be mine!

Mine to deny as it drains me dry.

Stole my control, lack thereof, therefore,

my strings keep growing back for more.

An uncut diamond made of the hardest coal.

She's a little bit cont — I'm a little bit rol.

The power of puss-uasion making me know my role,

through complete cont-inuous vag cont-rol.

Standing somewhere on Miracle Beach —

I can never, ever let you go.

Cryin' in the wild — won't you rescue me?

Don't you know she has total cont-rol?

THE POISON

You are the perfect poison,

a dark, dangerous touch that was meant to

be such a pretty poison that destroys and —

No antidote will do

The poison is you.

The cause/the reason/the incident/the accident.

I was/the doctor/you were/my experiment.

A concoction/confection/infection/condition.

A reaction/erection/connection/confession.

You are the perfect poison,

a dark, dangerous touch that was meant to

be such a pretty poison that destroys and —

No antidote will do

The poison is you.

The reason/is tainted/yet I'm still/unsatiated.

Lust/and decay/lonely love/bleeds away.

A delusion/prediction/confusion/reaction.

A deception/addiction/perversion/persuasion.

You are the perfect poison,

a dark, dangerous touch that was meant to

be such a pretty poison that destroys and —

No antidote will do

The poison is you.

No antidote will set me free

No…

The poison is me.

DON'T TOUCH ME

Her name was Beth, but I called her Mary —
because I liked that name better.
We compromised and said Mary Beth.
We met in June but called it September.

Yeah, yeah, can't catch me.
Now, now, don't touch me.

The time has come, you're a world away.
Bring back my turtleneck someday.
Now, I'm the Hulk, I was Bill Bixby.
I needed a vixen, and you were a pixie.

Yeah, yeah, can't catch me.

Walking in the gloaming, homeward,
late in the year.
You clawed at my pants,
and I,
at your brassiere.

Now, now, don't touch me.

You drove me away in your cursed hearse.
You left me here with an empty verse.
Don't worry, baby, maybe baby —
you caught me with nothing to say.

You. No, you.
You got me.

Yeah, yeah, can't catch me.
Now, now, don't touch me.

LOVER COME TO ME

Lover, come to me.
Lover, come to me.
Oh, love, won't you
come to me.

I've been waiting every day
since the day that you went away.
Oh, love... oh, lover, come to me.

You're the part of my lowly soul
that I can never, ever control.
My love — lover, come to me.

I've been sitting in the setting sun,

dreaming of the day that you will come.

Sweet love, oh, lover, come to me.

I've been dreaming in the darkest night —

shine your light and give me the right.

Oh, love, my lover, come to me.

By the fire of my pure desire,

in the name of the burning flame —

my love, sweet lover, come to me.

Lover, come to me.

Lover, come to me.

Oh, love, won't you

come to me.

Lover,

comfort me.

CHARMED + DANGEROUS

You can't tell me, baby, that I don't know how to love.

You can't say, baby, this hand don't fit you like a glove.

With my grips upon your hips,

tongue betwixt your lips —

to feel your charms, in my arms,

in my arms, up in arms.

Charmed and dangerous.

I will not be quieted,

while my love is unrequited.

It's you, it's true, I am aware
and I do declare:

Charming smarminess, indeed —
this dandy is going to give thee
a torn corset by my teeth.

You can't tell me, baby, that I don't know how to love.
You can't say, baby, this hand don't fit in you like a glove.

I will not be quieted,
while my love is unrequited.
It's you, it's true, I am aware,
and I dare declare:

With my grips upon your hips,
tongue betwixt your lips —
to feel your charms, in my arms,
in my arms, up in arms.

Charmed and dangerous.

BALLAD OF THE IRRESISTIBLE
& THE IMMOVABLE

She never knew there was a SuperCollider —

one programmed in me

and one inside her.

Inevitable clash of the titans —

you can feel it a comin'.

This is what happens

When an irresistible force meets an immovable object.

Deflect your heart to protect.

Collect my soul to connect.

Crackling in the ozone, the vibe is high.
The right time to intertwine is nigh.

You shot at me with your magnetic love gun.
I had my shields up and my mazer set to stun.

Soul-ular transformation.
Cardio-illogical disinformation.

She must be using a super-energy reverse polarizer.
Confound it — the batteries are dead
in my frequency harmon-arma-narma-nizer.

When an irresistible force meets an immovable object —
we have our hearts to protect.
I won't resist if you don't object
when an irresistible force meets an immovable object.

OUIJA BORED

I've not yet begun to become
As horrible as I will be —
I'm your October man.

Did you ever think
you could be that innocent again?

What we weave
is what we believe.
Genuine affectations.

The darkest part
of the darkest art

hidden deep
in a darkened heart.

Cloven-hoofed lass,
virgin of the universe.
The fact you made me feel anything
is quite something.

You're malicious.
Vicious and delicious.

Life isn't dead—
it's alive in the wiring.
I wanted to say *life is dead,*
but this is more inspiring.

Hiding behind the universal veil,
bare that crooked tooth when you smile.
The mask of hope can't hide
the eyes of despair.

Washing off the memories
of everything you almost destroyed.

I'm a whisper in your ear.
I'm your October man.

Abomination birthrite.
Eternal blood.
This darkness.

Strange toilets and nagging habits.
Kill yourself in a bathtub war
on the dark noon of a black Wednesday
after a late lunatic night.

Call to me.
I'm your October man.
Dead websites call to you
through the Ouija board for the living.

Heavy Meta thunder.

MICHELLE MCBRIDE

'O Michelle McBride,

who could ever not see?

I wish I knew you tonight,

for you I have yet to meet.

Into the autumn leaves we fall,

a little heart, a little tear.

Not really all that, after all —

opposite side of the mirror.

Michelle, Michelle, Michelle, Michelle —

who could ever not tell?

This has less to do with you,
and maybe more with me.
You're a portrait of someone who —
someone I've never seen.

Into the autumn leaves you fall,
a little heart, a little tear.
Not really all that, after all —
opposite side of the mirror.

'O Michelle McBride,
you're so far away.
There's no wonder to the why —
I just like the poetry of your name.

Into the autumn leaves I fall,
Michelle, Michelle.

A little heart, a little tear.
Michelle McBride.

Not really all that after all.
Michelle, Michelle.

Opposite side of the mirror.

Michelle McBride.

~To This Day~

† ☽ †

Untouchable, even by the face of time.

To this day there's something I can't always find.

I will find a place where I can't be hurt no more —

the scene of my destruction waits outside my door.

To this day, to this day.

Once there was the most dreamiest dream I'll ever know,

a kissing deep inside of me, massaging my soul.

Something so beautiful, I wish

I could have someone like her.

And now the only thing I know for sure

is I don't know for sure.

To this day, to this day.

Untouchable, even by the face of time.
Never could have thought I'd feel so fine.
I will find a place where teardrops fall no more.
My eyes are dry forever — and forever more.

To this day, to this day.

I can't cry.
To this day.

~*Crossed Streams*~

☽ † ☾

I get my hair cut,
and I even try to dress up, too.
Not that it makes a bit of difference to you.

You come over and hang on him,
your way of laughing in my face.
And I just can't put my pieces
back into their place.

I loved you.
You loved him.
He loved her,
and she loved me.
We never should have crossed the streams.

You flirt with him, and you think someday he'll be your
man.
Well, he's my friend, so I know and I understand.
He doesn't even like you — you just happened to be there.
Then there's me, over here, who just happened to care.

I loved you.
You loved him.
He loved her,
and she loved me.
We never should have crossed the streams.

It all started out in March of '95 —

playing hide and seek, you and your friend,

and me and mine.

I was hiding with her in the dark bathroom stall,

and before I knew it, we were up against the wall.

As we kissed, my eyes couldn't help but pretend it was

you.

I couldn't lie to my sight, no matter how hard I tried to.

So as I recollect, I laugh at taking it so rough.

I knew we'd lose both ways if we tried hard enough.

I loved you.

You loved him.

He loved her,

and she loved me.

We never should have crossed the streams.

The way it is, the way it seems —

we were warned never to cross the streams.

Untouchable, even by the face of time.

Never could have thought I'd feel so fine.

Please don't leave me for him,

and I won't leave you for her.

Trying to hide all the curious feelings

that you've stirred.

Michelle, Michelle, Michelle, Michelle —

my Michelle McBride.

A little heart, a little tear,

To this day, to this day.

To this day,

Our nights,

Are untouchable, even by the face of time.

ANGEL AT THE DAYS

I'm feelin' fine at the end of the day.
Don't walk all the way away.
Will you hold me like a bay-bay?
There was an angel at the days —
at the end of the day.

Turning lemons into lemonade.
Dark and light, yin and yang.
Sensitive souls, they cover their ears.
Kisses of cinnamon, cinnamon tears.

Lovesick, high-tech mash notes,
try to remember how they were wrote.
Dreaming of junior high kissing parties,
in a whirlwind cyclone of beauties.

Inhaling the scent of her trail
Breathing the breath of her exhale

I'm feelin' fine at the end of the day.
Don't walk all the way away.
Will you hold me like a bay-bay?
There was an angel at the days —
At the end of the day.

Closing like a soft bell
Ringing like a hard sell
I'm feeling time
At the end of the day

The end of days.

THE TIME AFTER TIME

I'll be back someday — but where am I now?
I will return for the kisses that I lost.
In a darkened dream, upon a silent cloud,
time and again, you're all that I want.

In the time after time, I'll find you again.
In the time after time, there will be no end.
In the time after time, I'll find you again.

I'll search the universe to find you, I swear.
Time after time, we'll always be there.

We've known each other in an ageless time,
and time after time, it's you I always try to find.

In the time after time, I'll find you again.
In the time after time, there will be no end.
In the time after time, I'll find you again.

In the garden of lifetimes, walking through the ages,
in my century-spanning writings, you're in all the pages.
When we meet again and are face to face,
eternity won't be such a lonely place.

In the time after time, I'll find you again.
In the time after time, there will be no end.
In the time after time, I'll find you again.

I am a traveler…
my search spans the galaxy…
I cannot die, I cannot die until I find…
what I'm looking for.

I WOULD IF I COULD

Been friends for a while,
and we used to talk about her.
I think about you, and I smile —
because before, I was just unsure.

I would if I could, but I can't.

Benefit friends for a while —
confession, depression, under pressure.
I think of you with a dry smile
when I think of what we did to her.

I would if I could, but I can't, so I won't.

Fate turns the tables on my fables.

She knew the song all along.

Ego rochambeau, crushed into half —

all she gave was a shrug, and a laugh.

I would if I could, but I can't.

I would,

If I could,

But I can't,

So I won't.

ONLY A MALL QUEEN

I've become a deadened angel.
The devil has sent me twins of evil.

We were beautiful and only sixteen,
and you were more than only a mall queen.

Half-baked memories of you are confined
to the backseat of my mind.
So many years and all between us —
I once wanted it, but enough's enough.

Can't look at you and make her mad.
Only a mall queen, the past be had.

Tear it to pieces, tear it apart —

without a cause, without a heart.

You've got your agenda, but not today.

You want to take my vitamins away.

I've got someone, I'm already taken.

I've told you before, if I'm not mistaken.

I'll remember your time and all I've seen —

lonely and only,

forever, a dead mall's queen.

GLAMOROUS & LOATHSOME

I am the darkness at the edge of town.
I am the happiness that can't be found.
I am the tape that can't be rewound.
I am the heart that has come unbound.

My bed is only half-full.
Too much self-pleasurevation.
Love is dirty, sex is worse.
If this is hell, then well-played.

Your shallow magnificence is an art unto itself.
While I'm emotionally in a state of giving zero flux.

Pure and bold to corrupt and old —
unscented senselessness.

Sexualized sexual eyes, sexual lies.
Whore d'oeuvres to sourly devour.
Aching minutes, crawling hours.
I fucked the past in the ass.

My sweet August entity,
tattooed in invisible ink.
Let sleeping prophets lie,
while arrested in the truth.

Save the habit, kick the planet.
Soiled eyes, fertile lies.
Damnation eyes.
Learn to be still… standing.

Sending regards to your ugly things.
Sleep with an angry leash,
and a renegade eyelash.

You look like death warmed over.

I look like death turned on.

All in my thrall.

I am the entity you can imitate.

I am the effigy you can immolate.

To think these chains

could hold one who cannot be restrained.

Looking your best in the worst of mirrors.

I'll make you smile, Glasgow-style.

You've seen me more naked

than I could ever be in the nude.

A sinister kind of urge —

for he's a Crowley good fellow.

These motherfucking snakes

on my plane of existence.

Entertain the angels

with this supercharged kind of life.

Time has made clowns of us all.

It was the one and only in the house of the lonely.

Hush, hush sweet harlot.

Suck me off, vampire.

Together we travel in haunted circles

of decay and satire.

Won't you wear my noose around your neck?

Moderation is okay in moderation —

but excess is best.

INSTRUMENTAL

HOLD THE REVOLUTION, EXTRA

CHEESE

And he sat there,
dead in his chair.
The revolution's on hold
in a post-ironic shootout.

The night is young,
just begun.
Taking unnamed pills,
medicated to my gills.

Constant constipated constellations,
a deadpan bedpan of prayers.

Tiny bubbles float and meet the air.
Heaven, let me in.

The revolution was never in your hands —
It was in your pants, in your past.
Get your shift together.
Get your shift in gear.

Where the lights go out,
and the revolution still waits —
fat and contented takes the day.

MY WORLD REVOLVES

Turning to your movement,
my world revolves.

Do what you want, where you are,
with who you be and what you got.
Do what you want, where you are,
with who you love and what you got.

Turning to your movement,
my world revolves.

Revelation, revolution.
Grand illusion, grand delusion.

Delusion, delusion, fair and true —
my world revolves,
with or without you.

Do what you want, where you are,
with who you be, with what you got.
Do what you want, where you are,
with who you love and not who is not.

Turning to your movement,
my world revolves.

NIKI, WITH ONE 'K'

You always go for the fixer-upper
and I might just be beyond repair,
ready to be razed without a cause,
condemned, without a care.

You were my girl from the north country,
always to be just a wannabe.
I could say your name—
but it's just too easy.

Why do I ever try?
You always want *that guy*.

Don't you always, N-I-K-I?
Yeah, you always, N-I-K-I.

Go for that goon with the raccoon eyes.
He's attracted you, along with the flies,
with his cute anger-management smile.
But he's got no skillz, got no style.

Maybe he can weld you a sheet metal flower,
give you all the mediocrity you can devour.
It's an all-you-can-eat buffet,
and you're accepting food stamps today.
It insults me that you'd mate that way.

Friend 'o mine you criticize
And say that I'm out 'o line
But did you ever think this thought
Maybe I want something like you got.

I'm not being harsh,
that's how I say "hello"
to those beneath me, below.
I was the better guy till she passed me by.

When it's my turn, will I return the spurn
or just take my place in line?

Why do I ever try?
You always want *that guy.*
Don't you always, N-I-K-I?
Yeah, you always, N-I-K-I.

You've been a good source of inspiration,
object of my right-handed perspirations.
Shouldn't be schooled by a foolish little tease,
like her boy toy, on my knees.

I do not want what I haven't got—
I bet you don't get that a lot.
Someday it's gonna be one-eighty degrees,
and my chilly reception will be
one to make you freeze.

Going, going, going—gone.
You're last night and I'm looking at dawn.
I'll stop my stopwatch from counting wasted time.
The bell has tolled, your last bell has chimed.

I'm starting it over, zero-zero-zero.

And you can fuck your next

zero-zero-zero hero.

Why do I ever try?

You always want *that guy*.

Don't you always, N-I-K-I?

Yeah, you always, N-I-K-I.

What do you have to say—

Niki, with one 'K'?

NOWHERE NEAR

You never know a city
until you walk it at night,
reading exquisite verse
in the neon night sky.

I've walked past creeping sidewalk shadow
and been bathed in the rays of TV glow —
pseudo-alleys and building cracks,
window reflections on railroad tracks,
rumbling, crumbling ramshackle shacks.

After years of Rip-Van-Winkling,
I walked into a kundalini of self,
feeling the weight of my fate —
long past my expiration date on the shelf.

The real me walked up and tapped my shoulder
and said, "Your only heart grew moldy and older."

I'm not comfortable at all with where time has brought us;
years of yearning crumbling to dust.
Everything I thought I knew has been turned and
reversed,
palpitating moments consumed with you,
burned with a curse.

I awoke from a dream thinking it was 1999,
then found myself caught in the cobweb of time.

Far from everything being fine,
everyone's dead and I'm alone,
a living ghost in my own home.

I'm going now to my '90s room to forget I'm here,

where my memories are living their lives —

and I am nowhere near.

HEARTS & BONES

I knock on the lid, you let me in.

Nighttime, our springtime,

has come once again.

Lay you down in your pillowtop coffin.

I ask, do you come here often?

I do — looking for you

in this darkness where only dead lovers do.

Lip meets lip, and we are now both quite stiff;

it's not just the chill,

it's my indomitable will.

Your touch is a bit cold,

flecked with mold.

You're a little dirty under the nails,

but still so damn exquisite —

you're always here waiting for my midnightly visit.

Your heart may have stopped,

but it still beats for me.

Faraway eyes, alive with love,

are all I see.

The night rolls on, bone on bone —

never to be gone,

never to be alone.

WHEN THE WORLD COMES TO AN END

Angel, come walk with me
for what will be all eternity.
When the wind cries across the land —
O, by me, you always will stand.

When the world comes to an end
I want to be, holding your hand.

Through all that is, was, and ever will be,
you'll be the first glimpse of heaven
and the last thing I will see.

As we walk, this one last night —
hand in hand, till the final blinding light.

When the world comes to an end
I want to be, holding your hand.

Angel, come now, don't you cry —
two true hearts will never say goodbye.
When comes our last moment to be true,
and my broken legs can no longer stand,
I will rise once more to stand beside you.

And I will be, holding your hand.

When the world comes to an end
I want to be, holding your hand.

Into oblivion,
I will be,
holding your hand.

I will be,
Holding your h—